Author:
Fiona Macdonald studied history at
Cambridge University, England, and at the
University of East Anglia. She has taught in
schools, adult education, and universities, and
is the author of numerous books for children.

Artist:
Bryan Beach

Editor:
Jacqueline Ford

© The Salariya Book Company Ltd MMXVIII

Published in Great Britain in 2018 by
The Salariya Book Company Ltd
25 Marlborough Place, Brighton BN1 1UB

ISBN-13: 978-0-531-22767-1 (lib. bdg.) 978-0-531-23077-0 (pbk.)

Published in 2018 in the United States
by Franklin Watts
An imprint of Scholastic Inc.

A CIP catalog record for this book is available
from the Library of Congress.

Printed and bound in China.
Printed on paper from sustainable sources.
1 2 3 4 5 6 7 8 9 10 R 27 26 25 24 23 22 21 20 19 18

SCHOLASTIC, FRANKLIN WATTS, and associated logos ar
trademarks and/or registered trademarks of Scholastic Inc.

Scholastic Inc., 557 Broadway, New York, NY 10012

PAPER FROM
SUSTAINABLE
FORESTS

The Science of OceanS

The Watery Truth About 72 Percent of Our Planet's Surface

written by
Fiona macDonald

Franklin Watts®
An Imprint of Scholastic Inc.

Illustrated by
Bryan Beach

Contents

Introduction

There's a lot of it around! Salty water, that is. The surface of our planet Earth is more than two-thirds (72 percent) covered by the stuff. We call small stretches of water "seas" and larger expanses "oceans," but they are all part of one gigantic World Ocean that is moving and changing—and affecting our lives—all the time. Without seas and oceans, we would not survive. But where did all this water come from? What does it do? Why do we need it? Read on, and find out more....

Water, Water Everywhere

Other planets have had oceans in the past. Scientists think that the oceans on Venus boiled away and dried up when the planet suffered from global warming.

The World Ocean contains 326 million cubic miles (1.3 billion cubic kilometers) of water—that's 97 percent of all the water on Earth. The rest is found in rivers and lakes, or frozen in ice sheets at the North and South Poles and as snow or glaciers on high mountains. Sailors, scientists, and geographers divide the World Ocean into five regional oceans: Pacific, Atlantic, Indian, Southern, and Arctic.

Oceans of the World

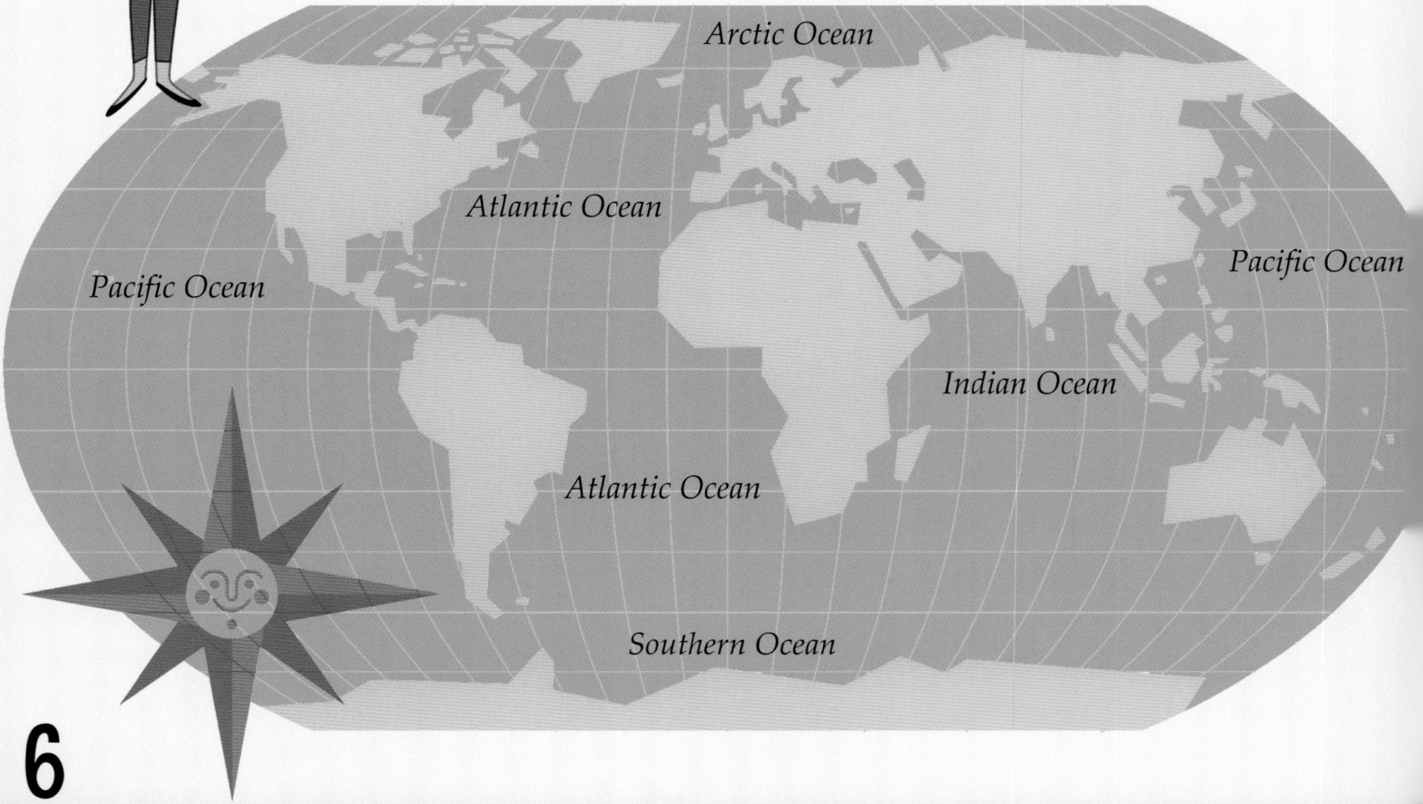

Arctic Ocean

Atlantic Ocean

Pacific Ocean

Pacific Ocean

Indian Ocean

Atlantic Ocean

Southern Ocean

Where Did Our Water Come From?

The oceans are as old as Earth itself: around 4.6 billion years old. No one knows for sure where the water came from, but scientists have suggested three possibilities:

1. Water was brought by meteorites as they crashed into the newly formed Earth.

2. Water fell to Earth from comets as they flew by.

3. Earth was formed when space dust and debris clustered together, trapping oxygen and hydrogen. The oxygen and hydrogen combined to create water.

Why are seas and oceans salty? Carbon dioxide in the atmosphere mixes with rain to form weak acid. This washes salty chemicals from Earth's rocks into ocean water.

!!!

Fascinating Fact

Our word *ocean* comes from the name of an Ancient Greek god (or monster), Oceanus. Greek myths described him as a giant snake surrounding Earth.

7

Ocean Floor

The ocean floor is part of Earth's crust—the outer layer of rocks forming the surface of our planet. The oceanic crust is thinner than the dry-land crust.

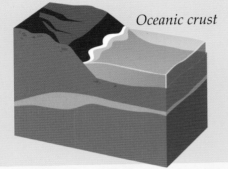

Dry-land crust

Oceanic crust

The deepest place anywhere in the oceans is the Mariana Trench, in the western Pacific Ocean near the island of Guam. The bottom of the trench is an amazing 6.8 miles (11 km) below the surface of the ocean.

Ocean Zones

The ocean is both very wide and very, very deep. On average, it's about 12,000 feet (3,700 meters) from waves on the ocean surface to rocks on the ocean floor. That's nearly as deep as America's Rocky Mountains are high. The ocean is shallowest close to land, and deepest in trenches—steep narrow valleys in the ocean floor. Scientists divide ocean waters into zones. Shallow water zones are warmed and lit by the sun's rays. But light and heat from the sun can't reach deep water zones; they are extremely dark and cold.

650 feet (200 m)   *Sunlight Zone*

3,000 feet (900 m)   *Twilight Zone*

13,000 feet (4,000 m)   *Midnight Zone*

Trench

Under the Sea

Water in the upper zones of oceans presses down on the water below it. The deeper the water, the greater the pressure. Just like on dry land, there are hills, mountains, valleys, and plains on the ocean floor.

There are even underwater volcanoes, called seamounts. Scientists have discovered over 60,000 seamounts—many of which are alive, and erupting!

Mid-ocean ridges form because Earth's rocky crust has broken into huge pieces, called tectonic plates. As these plates rub against each other, hot rock from deep within Earth rises to fill the gaps, then cools and solidifies to form new ridges.

Mid-ocean ridge

Mid-Ocean Ridges

Massive rows of undersea mountains, called mid-ocean ridges, stretch along the ocean floor for over 40,000 miles (65,000 km). That's much longer than any mountain ridge on Earth's surface.

Fascinating Fact

The first people to reach the bottom of the Mariana Trench were the crew of the bathyscape (an ultra deep-sea vessel) *Trieste*, in 1960. Traveling at 2 miles per hour (3.2 kph), the dangerous descent took 4 hours and 47 minutes.

Going down!…

Anatomy of a Wave

As the wind blows over the ocean, waves are raised above the surface to form high crests tipped with white foam. Between each wave, there is a trough (hollow). The distance from one wave crest to the next is called the wave length.

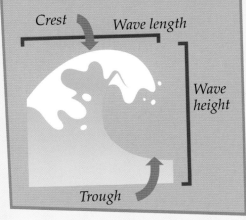

Crest
Wave length
Wave height
Trough

Violent winds such as hurricanes cause storm surges. Water pushed by winds piles up in huge waves when it reaches the shore, causing floods and wrecking buildings.

Waves and Swells

The ocean is always moving, never still. Its upper zones are disturbed by tiny ripples, wild waves, and huge tsunamis. Oceans also rise and fall in smooth, rhythmic swells. What causes all this water to move? Waves, ripples, and swells all happen when energy passes through the water. Usually, the energy comes from the wind. A gentle breeze makes tiny ripples; a fierce gale makes huge waves. Amazingly, no two waves are ever the same.

Surf's up!

Even after a wind has died down and no big waves disturb the surface, the ocean still keeps moving. The smooth, steady rise and fall of the water is called a swell.

How Winds Make Waves

Energy to make waves passes into water when winds push against it. The stronger the wind, the more energy it carries into the water.

The fetch (the distance over which the wind blows) is also important. The longer the fetch is, the bigger the waves will be.

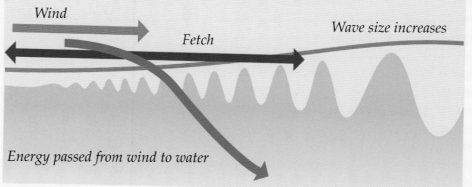

Wind

Fetch

Wave size increases

Energy passed from wind to water

ry It Yourself

ill a plastic bowl halfway ith water. Blow on it or tap ne side gently; this will pass nergy into the water and ake waves. Observe how he waves spread through the ater in the bowl. They don't ust stay close to the place hey started. Waves and swells pread through the ocean in he same way.

Tsunamis

Energy to make waves can also come from earthquakes on the ocean floor or erupting seamounts (underwater volcanoes). The energy these release causes massive waves, known as tsunamis, that rise

up like walls of water. Tsunamis can devastate towns and villages along the coast and travel far inland. The tallest wave ever measured was 1,719 feet (524 m) high, at Lituya Bay, Alaska, in 1958.

Tidal Bulges

The pull of gravity is strongest on the side of Earth closest to the moon. So more water is pulled there, creating a tidal bulge. On the side farthest from the moon, the moon's gravitational pull is at its weakest, causing a matching tidal bulge there.

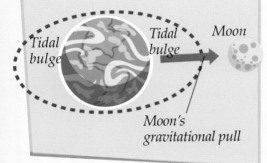

Tidal bulge

Tidal bulge

Moon

Moon's gravitational pull

Tides

There's another reason why seas and oceans are always moving. Every day, water levels around the coast rise and fall in regular patterns known as tides. These are very long, slow-moving waves caused by gravity: when massive objects such as the moon and the sun pull less massive things, such as water, toward them. When the crest of a tide wave reaches the shore, the water level there rises. When the trough of a tide wave reaches the shore, the water level falls. We see the ocean slowly rolling in closer, then ebbing away (retreating). That's awesome!

The pull of gravity depends on the mass of objects—and also how far away they are. The moon is much smaller than the sun but much closer to Earth. So its effect on tides is stronger.

We'd better keep an eye on the tide!

Low tide

High tide

High and Low Tides

In most places, there are high and low tides approximately twice a day. But because the moon takes 24 hours and 50 minutes to orbit Earth, high tides and low tides happen every 12 hours and 25 minutes. This means that the precise times of high and low tides, measured by the 24-hour clock, change every day.

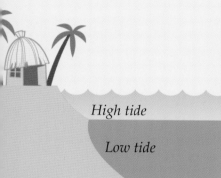

High tide

Low tide

In the past, sailors liked to set out to sea on an *ebb* (retreating) tide. It carried their boats safely away from the shore, whichever way the wind was blowing. The sailors used the power of the moving water to make a speedy start to their voyage.

Spring and Neap Tides

Tides are not the same all year round. When the sun, moon, and Earth are in line with each other, the pull of their gravity on ocean water is strongest and tides are highest. These are called spring tides, and happen twice a month, at full moon and new moon.

When the sun, moon, and Earth are not in line, the pull of their gravity is not so strong. So ocean water is not pulled up as much, and tides are lower. The lowest tides are called neap (weak) tides. They happen twice a month, when we see a half-moon in the night sky.

Spring tide

Neap tide

Why It Happens

Have you heard of rip currents? They can be very dangerous to swimmers, dragging them far out to sea. They are currents (streams of water) formed by tide waves breaking on the shore, then ebbing. Rip currents flow back out to sea at up to 8 feet (2.5 m) per second. That's faster than an Olympic champion swimmer!

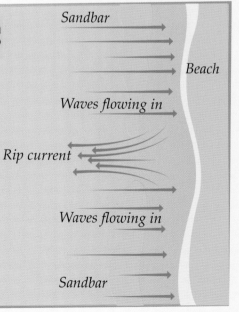

Sandbar

Beach

Waves flowing in

Rip current

Waves flowing in

Sandbar

Warm and Cold Currents

Deep-Water Currents

In icy regions, ocean water is colder and denser (heavier for its size) than water from near the equator. It's also saltier, because water that freezes as icebergs leaves its salt in the ocean. This cold, dense water sinks down, where it flows as deep-water currents. Warmer surface water then flows in to replace it.

Streams of water—known as currents—flow within seas and oceans. They are found at the water's surface and deep down. Surface currents are warm; deep-water currents are cold. Just like waves, they are always moving. Surface currents are caused mostly by the wind. Warm winds from lands close to the equator blow toward cold regions at the North and South Poles. They pass energy into ocean waters as they move, making surface currents flow in the same direction. Deep-water currents are caused by differences in temperature, density, and saltiness in different regions of the ocean.

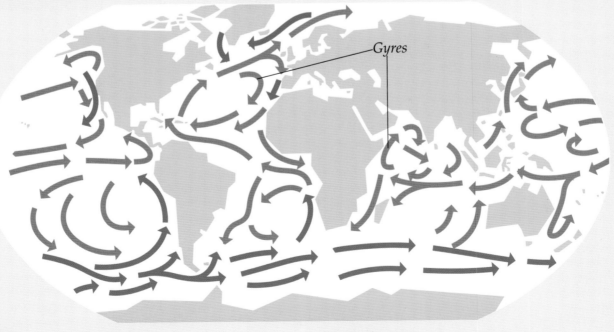

Gyres

14

→ Warm surface currents   → Cold surface currents

The Global Conveyor Belt

Ocean currents are linked together in a giant circulation of water known as the Global Conveyor Belt. Very slowly, warmer water from surface currents sinks down into the ocean while colder water from deep currents rises up. The Conveyor Belt is so vast and moves so slowly that it takes a drop of water 1,000 years to go from one end to the other.

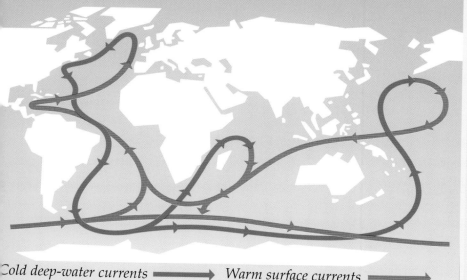

Cold deep-water currents →   Warm surface currents →

The Gulf Stream

The Gulf Stream is one of the strongest warm-water currents. It flows from the Gulf of Mexico, along the east coast of North America, then across the Atlantic Ocean to the west coast of Europe. Its fast-flowing waters helped European explorers make daring voyages—and sail back home safely again.

As ocean surface currents flow north and south, they are pushed sideways by forces generated when Earth spins around. This helps create circling currents, called gyres. You can see these on page 14.

Can You Believe It?

Without the warm waters of the Gulf Stream current, the British Isles and nearby regions of western Europe might be as cold as northern Canada.

Oceans, Winds, and Weather

Polar Cold

Regions close to the North and South Poles receive less heat energy from the sun than places close to the equator. This is because the sun's rays shine on them at a low angle, spreading heat energy thinly across a vast area.

45°
90°
45°

Earth is the only place we know—so far—where life exists. And that's thanks to our oceans. Earth's seas and oceans provide the water that all living things need to survive. They also control Earth's temperature, by spreading the heat energy Earth receives from the sun more evenly across its surface. How do they do this? By moving large amounts of heat in ocean currents, and by creating winds—moving currents of air. Winds carry heat energy from the ocean high into the sky, and from warm regions to cool ones. And they never stop blowing!

Warm water vapor evaporating from oceans is the biggest cause of global warming. But dark clouds formed from water vapor also shield Earth from the sun's rays, and keep it cooler. A balanced system!

Evaporation

The ocean stores vast amounts of heat energy from the sun. But warm ocean water evaporates (turns to vapor) and rises into the sky. This process takes energy away from Earth's surface, and cools it.

Clouds

Water vapor

Warm oc
surface

Convection

Warm air is less dense than cold air, so it rises and floats above it. When warm air cools, it becomes denser, and sinks down again. It's easy to see how this happens in a room with a heater. But the same process—called convection—happens across the world's oceans, too (see right).

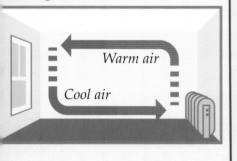

Warm air

Cool air

Warm air can carry more water vapor than cold air. So warm, rising winds bring rain, but cold, sinking winds are dry. Regions of Earth where winds are warm and wet have hot, rainy weather. Where cold dry winds blow, there are often deserts.

Global Winds

As warm air rises up above the oceans, and colder air sinks down, convection currents are created in Earth's atmosphere, all around the globe. We call these air currents winds. Ocean winds also blow across Earth's surface from warm regions to cooler ones. Sailors long ago observed that these winds blew in regular, predictable patterns. They called them "trade" winds, because they "trod" a steady path across the ocean.

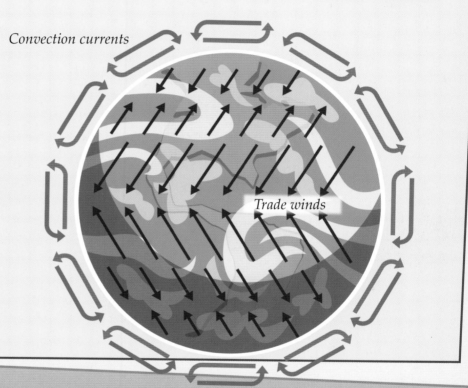

Convection currents

Trade winds

Why It Happens

Why does the ocean look blue? Sunlight shining on Earth contains all seven colors of the rainbow. But the ocean absorbs them all, except blue. It reflects that back into our eyes.

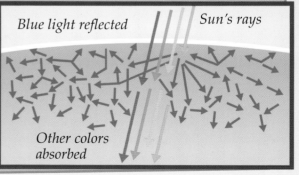

Blue light reflected

Sun's rays

Other colors absorbed

How Do Hurricanes Happen?

Rising warm air causes low surface pressure above the ocean. New warm wet ocean winds rush in to fill it. The winds curve into a funnel shape as Earth rotates. They spin faster and faster, rising high, sucking up more water vapor and creating fearsome tropical storms.

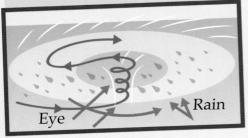

Eye   Rain

Ocean Extremes

For most of the time, ocean winds and sea currents work well together. But sometimes the processes that give us normal ocean winds and weather can generate enormous forces that lead to deadly extremes. Giant storms starting over the oceans wreck ships, destroy coastal regions, cause travel chaos, and kill thousands of people and animals. Changes in ocean currents also cause floods, droughts, famines, and other types of destruction. Let's look at two examples of ocean extremes: hurricanes and El Niño.

A hurricane is the name given to killer storms in the Atlantic Ocean. They are called cyclones in the Indian Ocean and typhoons in the Pacific.

Superstorms

Whirling hurricane storm clouds can rise 9 miles (14.5 km) high into the atmosphere and measure 60 miles (96.5 km) across.

Roaring hurricane wind speeds can reach nearly 200 miles per hour (320 kph). Violent hurricane rainfall can total 4 feet (1.2 m) in just one day.

El Niño happens when easterly winds that blow across the Pacific Ocean weaken. Most years, they guide a current of cold water rising from the deep ocean. Without the winds, it changes direction and is replaced by warmer water.

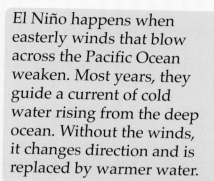

Eye

Storm clouds driven by winds

El Niño

This is the name given to changes in currents in the Pacific Ocean. It happens every five to seven years. A huge mass of warm surface water (shown yellow, below) moves toward the west coast of South America. It brings storms, droughts, and famine, kills fish and sea creatures, and bleaches coral reefs.

Fascinating Fact

When El Niño warm water appears, it releases so much energy into the atmosphere that trade winds weaken or change direction. Pacific storms move east. There can also be record high temperatures in Australia, drought in Africa and India, floods in South America, chilly clouds in the southern United States, and strangely warm weather in Canada.

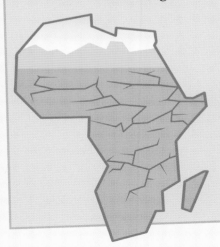

The Water Cycle

The oceans contain most (97 percent) of the world's water. But the water does not stay there all the time. Instead, it floats through the air as clouds and trickles in streams across dry land. It drifts as fog, drops as rain, sparkles as snowflakes, and runs as rivers before returning to the oceans. Together, all these movements are called the water cycle. A molecule of water typically takes about 10 days to complete the whole journey, unless it freezes solid in an ice sheet or gets trapped underground.

About 2 percent of the world's water is frozen in mountain glaciers and polar ice caps. If our climate changed, and this ice melted, ocean levels would rise and low-lying countries would vanish below the waves. Many coastal cities, such as Miami, Florida, might also disappear.

Most water in the water cycle comes from the oceans, by evaporation. But about 10 percent is passed into the air through plants, in a process called transpiration. A big tree can transpire up to 33,000 gallons (125,000 liters) of water in a year.

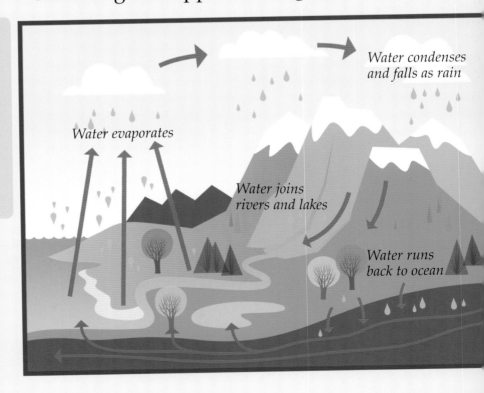

Water condenses and falls as rain

Water evaporates

Water joins rivers and lakes

Water runs back to ocean

How Does It Work?

It takes heat energy from the sun to make the water cycle run smoothly. When you heat a liquid such as water, it changes to a vapor (gas). When a vapor cools, it condenses back into a liquid. When a liquid is cooled to low temperatures, it freezes. Liquid water freezes to become ice.

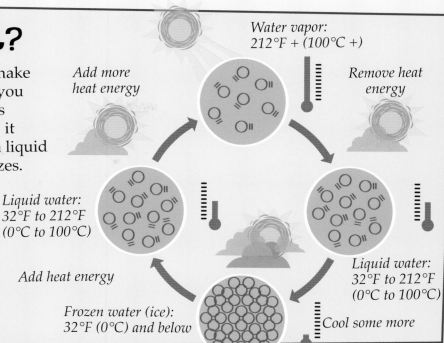

Water vapor: 212°F + (100°C +)

Add more heat energy

Remove heat energy

Liquid water: 32°F to 212°F (0°C to 100°C)

Liquid water: 32°F to 212°F (0°C to 100°C)

Add heat energy

Cool some more

Frozen water (ice): 32°F (0°C) and below

Try It Yourself

Very carefully, put a clean, dry plastic bag over a leafy plant in a flowerpot. The soil in the pot should be moist but not too wet. After a day or so, you should see little drops of water on the inside of the plastic bag. This water has been pulled up from the soil by the plant, and passed out through the leaves. That's transpiration!

Floating in the Air

Clouds, mist, and fog store almost 3,100 cubic miles (12,900 cubic km) of water evaporated from oceans, in the form of tiny droplets. These droplets are not heavy enough to fall as rain unless they can join together.

Small droplets join together to form large raindrops

21

Bony Fish

Fish are some of the oldest living creatures on Earth. They evolved 500 million years ago—long before humans, or dinosaurs. They have bony skeletons, use fins to propel themselves, and have gills to breathe underwater. All are covered with a protective layer of slime; most are cold-blooded.

22

Ocean Life

Our oceans are the richest environment anywhere on Earth. Amazing sea creatures live in every part of them, from icy waters at the poles to warm waters in the tropics. Ocean wildlife has adapted to suit many different surroundings: the open sea, coral reefs, shallow rock pools, or the deep, dark ocean floor. Each different zone has its own ecosystem. The plants and creatures there have evolved to live together, making the best use of the food and shelter they find in the ocean waters around them.

Sunlight Zone: sharks, whales, bony fish, mammals, coral, plants

Twilight Zone: octopus, squid, jellyfish

Midnight Zone: worms, snails, crabs; no plants

Deep trenches—giant crustaceans, sea cucumbers, jellyfish, bacteria

Cartilaginous Fish

Sharks have tough, flexible cartilage instead of bones. They catch their food using rows of sharp teeth; when one tooth falls out, another moves forward to replace it. They can swim 60 miles per hour (96 kph)! Rays are related to sharks, but have flattened, kite-shaped bodies, with mouths, nostrils, and gills on the underside.

Marine Mammals

These are warm-blooded creatures that feed their babies on the mother's milk. They include the largest creatures on Earth (whales) and some of the most intelligent (dolphins), as well as otters, seals, and sea lions. Many marine mammals have blubber (fat) under their skin to keep them warm in icy oceans. Others have fur for warmth.

Mollusks and Crustaceans

There are 50,000 different mollusks, such as squid, octopus, and oysters. Some have shells, some don't, but their bodies all have three parts: a head (with eyes and brain), a food-digesting organ, and a foot. Crustaceans have an exoskeleton (hard outer covering), feelers, eyes, a brain, and a stomach. They include crab, shrimp, and lobsters, which are valued as food.

Why It Happens

Fish need oxygen to survive. So they gulp ocean water and push it out through gills on each side of their neck (somewhat like filters). The gills let oxygen in the water pass into the fishes' blood.

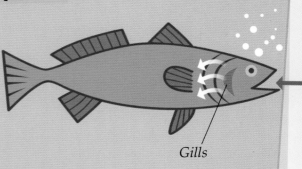

Gills

23

How We Use the Oceans

Food From the Sea

For thousands of years, people living by the ocean have caught fish and other sea creatures to eat. In the past, they used lines, spears, and nets. Today, ships with huge underwater shovels scoop up the catch.

A good catch today!

We rely on oceans for many important natural resources, from food to fuels, building materials, jewelry, and fertilizers. We use the oceans as a highway. Most of the world's cargoes are carried onboard ships. We hide weapons in deep waters, patrol the seas around our coasts for defense, and send warships across the oceans to attack enemies with planes, drones, and missiles. We lay communications cables across the ocean floor, bounce radio waves off the ocean surface, and station TV transmission satellites high above it.

Glowing, shimmering pearls are produced by oysters (mollusks). They are some of the world's most beautiful jewels.

Around 90 percent of the world's cargo (measured by weight) is carried by sea.

Undersea Energy

Since the 19th century, we have relied on fossil fuels (coal, oil, and natural gas) for power. At first, these were mined on dry land. But as land-based supplies became scarce, prospectors looked for fossil fuel deposits under the sea. Today, oil rigs can operate in ocean waters up to nearly 10,000 feet (3,000 m) deep.

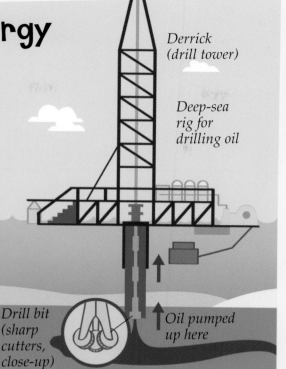

Derrick (drill tower)

Deep-sea rig for drilling oil

Drill bit (sharp cutters, close-up)

Oil pumped up here

Some of the first settlements built by early modern humans were beside seas and oceans. Prehistoric peoples sheltered in caves, and gathered shellfish along the shore.

Sports and Recreation

"Oh, we do like to be beside the seaside!" From kayaking at a sandy beach to sailing, scuba diving, and around-the-world cruises, we use the oceans to exercise and have fun.

Why It Happens

Today, the race is on to find new types of nonpolluting renewable energy. Tidal turbines work somewhat like wind turbines, but underwater. The energy in the ocean's currents turns the turbines, which generate electricity.

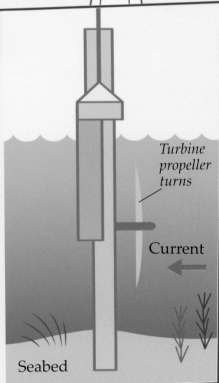

Turbine propeller turns

Current

Seabed

Dying Coral

Coral reefs look like beautiful underwater gardens. They are made of skeletons from coral (tiny sea creatures), plus algae—and are threatened by global warming.

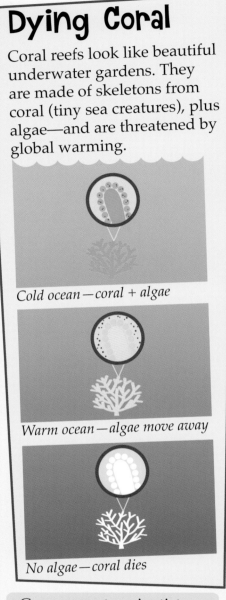

Cold ocean—coral + algae

Warm ocean—algae move away

No algae—coral dies

Governments, scientists, charities, and campaigning groups are all trying to save our oceans. We can help, too, by respecting our own environment, wherever we are.

Oceans in Danger

Once pure and clean, the world's oceans are now dirty, polluted, and in danger. We humans are to blame. Thoughtlessly we have caught too many fish, killed too many whales and sharks, let sewage, oil, and farm chemicals run into ocean waters, and dumped trash of all kinds into the seas around the coast. Global warming has destroyed habitats; drilling, mining, and building have wrecked underwater ecosystems. Today, we understand that oceans—the largest biome (living space) on Earth—are a fragile environment. And they need protecting!

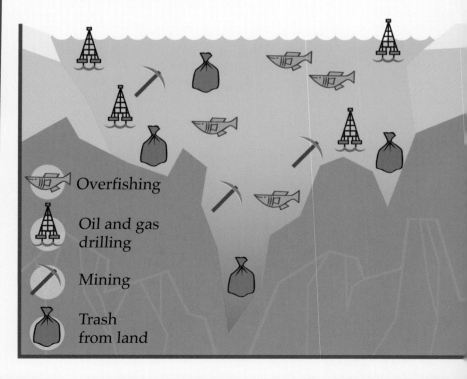

Overfishing

Oil and gas drilling

Mining

Trash from land

Oil Spills

Each year, there are thousands of spills from ships and drilling rigs. Oil and chemicals pour into the ocean. Spills kill fish, birds, and other sea creatures. They pollute fisheries, wreck tourist beaches, and destroy coastal communities. The damage they do lasts for a very long time.

The Great Pacific Garbage Patch is a vast area of ocean polluted by plastic, chemicals, and other trash thrown overboard from ships or dumped at sea. Ocean currents have collected this debris together. No one has yet found a way to clean it up.

Help!

Killer Hooks

Long-liner boats drag 62-mile (100 km) fishing lines with jagged hooks through ocean waters. Experts say that these hooks kill 40,000 sea turtles, 300,000 seabirds, millions of sharks, and thousands of marine mammals every year. They want long-line fishing to be banned.

Try It Yourself

You can help save the oceans by recycling trash whenever possible, or throwing it away carefully. If you get the chance to join an organized cleanup of a beach or waterway, please do it!

Earth's Final Frontier?

To the Deepest Place on Earth

In 2012, explorer James Cameron piloted the Deepsea Challenger to the bottom of the Mariana Trench. The water pressure squeezed the extremely strong Challenger so much that it got smaller!

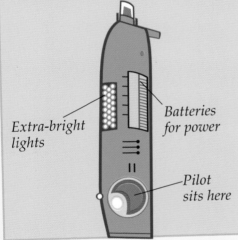

Extra-bright lights

Batteries for power

Pilot sits here

Exploring the deepest ocean zones is difficult, dangerous, and expensive. Total darkness and crushing water pressure make them a very hostile place for visitors, so there's a lot we don't yet know about them. But technology has made it possible to launch daring investigations, and to find strange and surprising life-forms. These new discoveries increase our scientific knowledge. They also encourage us to become "ocean aware" so we value the beauty, diversity, and importance of our amazing oceans.

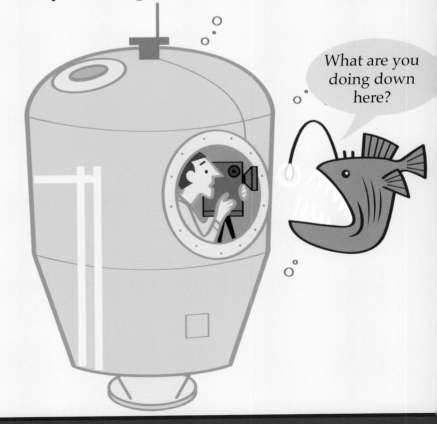

What are you doing down here?

Strange but true! We know less about some parts of the oceans on our own planet Earth than about the surface of the moon.

Solving an Age-Old Mystery

In the past, sailors told fantastic tales of ferocious deep-sea monsters such as giant squid (mollusks) that dragged sailing ships underwater. For centuries, no one believed the sailors, but in 2013, scientists using special deep-water cameras filmed real-life giant squid in the ocean near Japan.

Strangers of the Deep

Scientists send ROVs (robotic underwater vehicles) to explore the hidden depths of the ocean. They can beam back video footage of newly discovered underwater life and collect samples for study in laboratories. This polynoid worm was first sighted in 2010, 1.5 miles (2.5 km) below sea level, in the Atlantic Ocean.

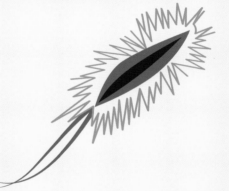

French scientist and explorer Jacques Cousteau (1910–1997) was an underwater hero. By making some of the first-ever films about marine wildlife, he revealed the wonders of the oceans to millions of people.

Can You Believe It?

In 1977, explorers discovered hydrothermal vents: smoky "chimneys" above cracks in the ocean floor. The vents are extremely hot (around 700°F/370°C), very dark, and surrounded by chemicals. In spite of this, scientists have found 750 new types of sea creatures—crabs, shrimps, snails, worms, and bacteria—that have evolved to survive there.

29

Glossary

Algae Tiny living creatures, related to seaweed, that grow in ponds, rivers, and oceans.

Bathyscape Extra-strong vessel designed for deep-water exploration.

Carbon dioxide A gas produced by living things and by burning fossil fuels.

Comet Giant ball of frozen gas, rock, and space dust that orbits the sun.

Convection The circular flow of heat energy from a warm place to a cold place in liquids and gases.

Crust Layer of rocks forming the outer surface of planet Earth.

Current Stream of water flowing through the ocean.

Denser Heavier (having more mass) for its size.

Ebb Flow away. An ebb tide is a tide that flows away from the shore.

El Niño Changes to currents flowing in the Pacific Ocean. El Niño causes abnormal weather in many parts of the world.

Evaporate Turn into vapor (gas).

Exoskeleton Hard outer covering of a living creature, such as a lobster or a crab.

Fetch Distance that a wind blows over the surface of seas and oceans.

Fossil fuels Fuels formed from the remains of living things: coal, oil, and natural gas.

Gills Parts of a fish. Oxygen from seawater passes through gills into the fish's blood to keep it alive.

Gyre Current that flows in a circle

Hurricane Giant, tropical storm with extreme winds and rainfall. Formed over seas and oceans. (Also known as cyclone or typhoon.)

Hydrogen A gas that combines with oxygen to form water.

Hydrothermal vents Very hot "chimneys" rising from cracks in the ocean floor.

Meteorite Lump of rock from a comet, asteroid, or other space body that crashes into planet Earth.

Mid-ocean ridge Long line of underwater mountains formed when tectonic plates move away from each other.

Oxygen Gas essential for life on Earth. When combined with hydrogen, it forms water.

Rip current Dangerous current that flows rapidly from the shore out to sea.

Seamount Underwater mountain, formed by volcanic eruptions.

Storm surge Sudden dangerous rise in sea level caused by a violent storm. Often floods coastal areas.

Swell Slow, smooth waves that occur when ocean water stores energy from the winds blowing across it.

Tectonic plates Massive sections of Earth's crust and the layer of rock just below it (the upper mantle). Tectonic plates move very slowly.

Tide Regular rises and falls of sea level caused by the pull of gravity of the moon and sun and the orbital motion of Earth around the moon or sun.

Trade winds Winds that blow regularly and steadily across warm oceans on either side of the equator.

Transpiration When plants pull water up from the soil and pass it out into the air.

Tsunami Huge, powerful wave, usually caused by an earthquake or volcano erupting underwater.

Turbine Machine with turning parts that "capture" energy from moving liquid or gas so that it can be used to generate power.

World Ocean Collective name for all the seas and oceans on planet Earth.

Index